18 Years Of Solitude

Moné Cohen

18 YEARS OF SOLITUDE.
Copyright © 2020. Moné Cohen. All Rights Reserved.

Printed in the United States of America.

No portion of this book may be reproduced, stored in a retrieval system, or transmitted in any form or by any means, except for brief quotations in printed reviews, without the prior written permission of DayeLight Publishers or Moné Cohen.

ISBN: 978-1-949343-93-9

*I dedicate this book to
all teenage girls,
especially to Rebecca,
Nashieka, Heather,
Ketoni and Tahfria.*

Acknowledgments

My paramount acknowledgement is to God who created me and has kept me through trying times. I am here today solely because of the saving and redeeming power of Jesus Christ.

My heart of gratitude goes out to my mom, who is my biggest fan; thank you for believing in me first, so I could believe in myself.

To my mentor, Robert Spence, your good advice and motivation keeps me going.

To Garland Drake and Stephen D.N. Stanberry who critiqued my manuscript and gave me suggestions, I sincerely thank you.

To all those who continue to believe in me and read my work, I thank you.

Special acknowledgment to Romaine Allen-Johnson, whose question: "When will you publish the book?" has pushed me to turn a dream into a reality.

Finally, I must thank Crystal Daye and DayeLight Publishers for publishing and propelling my work.

Thank you all.

TABLE OF CONTENTS

Acknowledgments v
Introduction 1
Preface 3
    Foreword 5
    Shanae 6
    Precious Jewel 8
    Fallen 10
    The Rain 12
    Ghetto Pressure 13
    Unfair Yet? 15
    Pain 17
    Trapped In Our Minds 20
    Second Priority 22
    Limited 24
    In His Mind 25
    Poverty 27
    Broken Hearted 28
    Sleep 31
    My Story 33
    Unbreakable Bond 35
    The Crush 36
    Insecurity 38
    Sky Of Battle 40

Listening to Music?	41
Happiness Is For Humans	44
Night's Rest	47
Cold	50
Compliment	52
Struggling On	54
From My Distance	56
The Album	58
Hopeless	60
Mental Slavery	62
Declaring The Promise	63
Self- Righteous	66
Joyful Noise	70
Refuse	72
Cry	75
The Brick Wall	77
IDK	78
Limbo	84
The Last Prayer	86
Reflection	89
Unforeseen	90
Dreams	92
Black Rain	94
Her Mind	96
Flirt	98
The Black Woman's Heart	99
Ridden	101
Let Me Be	102
This Melody	103
Anger	105
About the Author	107

Introduction

I have always had a problem expressing my feelings. I can speak about what I know in a sensible manner for hours. However, when it relates to how I feel, I just can't find the words to speak, so I started writing little rhymes of what I could not say. I started getting better at expressing how I felt through rhymes.

I can also express myself through dancing, singing, sign language, playing the keyboard, and drawing - basically through any other medium other than speaking about how I feel. I embraced my diverse ways of expressing and applauded myself for getting the emotions out, instead of bottling them in.

The dancing, drawing, and writing decoded what my heart was trying to say. I became aware of what I was feeling. I started to understand myself better. Then I realized no one had heard my poems, seen me dance or heard me play. I had been expressing, but only to myself.

PREFACE

I was a very active child while growing up. I was very adventurous, outspoken, and playful. When I was nine years old, my younger sister died and that was my first and, possibly, the most impactful traumatic experience I had. As a child, the feeling of loss was hard to articulate; all the pain and emotions I felt, I just could not express verbally. I took to writing. This produced my first poem "Shanae," where I expressed how I felt about the death of my sister. Ever since then I had grown more introverted and withdrawn. I had chosen writing as my main mode of expression; thus, the birth of a ravishing poet and a graceful writer.

At the age of fourteen I had another crisis in my life and my writing took to a new dimension. Between the ages of twelve to fourteen, I mostly toyed with emotions in my poems, bringing scenarios from my imagination to life or speaking about the reality around me; whereas at fifteen years of age, my poems became more emotional and soul touching. I had been deeply hurt and so I delved deeper to pour out the emotions in my writing. I must admit that in these pages lie some dark truth but there are also some colourful stories and some daunting lines. This is the story of my life, all penned out in ugly words and beautiful lines. This is the documentation of my journey from childhood into adolescence.

I fear that without these words I would have become a bitter, self-destructive person. This (18 Years of Solitude) is the score – the melody to all the songs I have sung in the first eighteen years of my life. As the title suggests these eighteen years were predominantly characterized by solitude, which has made me into the person I am today and continues to mould me.

Foreword

Expression
What I express
These thoughts are not compressed
Not made by requests
These words I profess
And confess are more or less
Those of my feelings, yes
My weariness and dreariness
Of my failures and success
Conquests, regrets
Of acceptance and neglect
Negligence of the intelligence
Of other people's minds
Not pieces of intellectual property
They have left behind
No repetition of speeches
To which my ears have been inclined
No, not a sign!
For these words are
Wholly and Solely and
Forever Mine

Shanae

Shanae was my sister
Someone who was so kind to me
One day there was news
I wondered what it would be

My sister died
On July 21, 2007
I wondered where she had gone
She was gone to heaven

Blood cancer had
Taken her away
Not even a goodbye
I got to say

I loved my sister,
I was kind to her
And she was kind to me
My heart is still broken

And it is sad to see

Sometimes I feel sick
Sometimes I feel sad
Every time I hear the word cancer
I get really mad

We were like twins
So alike
Until to Leukaemia
You lost the fight
Without you in my life
I feel a great loss
You were my best friend
From when I was a lass

No matter where I turn
To the West or to the East
I will never find you
Because you are resting in peace

Right now, I wish
I could hold your hand
But you're in the grave
So, rest on.[1]

---

[1] My first poem ever about the death of my sister. Written when I was nine years old.

Precious Jewel

It's three years now
Almost four and
I can't believe that
I'm still pouring
Over this thing
That happened so long ago

I should have known
That you were leaving
Although it was grieving
It was relieving
To see you stop feeling
All that pain
And be happy again

But I'm restless
Without you by my side
Your spirit
I use for my guide
Your love I know

Would never beguile
You were an angel
Sent from above
A precious jewel beloved

Still grieving
Now that I remember
All the fun
We had in December
No joy I fully share in
Because you're not here

Seems like yesterday
We were having fun
Never knew that
You'd soon be gone
Now I'm sitting here
All alone

I know that
One day I will
See you again
In the midst of
Our family and friends
And I'll remember you
Just like I used to
An angel sent from above
A precious jewel beloved.[2]

---

[2] Poem commemorating the death of my sister. Written when I was twelve years old.

Fallen

Cramps make me moody
But pain makes me a woman
The pain
It relapses
It penetrates
It stings
To make me stronger
To make me harder to hurt
But somehow not strong enough
To make me realise
You will never care
Never love
Never need me again
But I want you
I need you!
I'll love you
Forever
But will always regret the day
I let you go
Out of my arms,
And you walked away

And never even
Looked back
To realize
I've fallen[3]

---

[3] Written when I was thirteen years old.

The Rain

The rain is a blessing
To my soul
It brings me joy
And what hope to behold

The rain is precious
Something I can't replace
At any time or place
It soothes my pain
And makes me think again

It compels me to
Give thanks to God
For all that I see
But most of all
It makes me believe
In hope for you and me.[4]

---

[4] Written when I was thirteen years old.

Ghetto Pressure

Do you even know
What it is to face real ghetto pressure?
When every day you get up
To eat dumpling and butter
When you can't afford the mackerel
Have to credit from Miss Sherill
At the corner shop

Do you really know
What it is to be fatherless?
Trying to help mommy
To get out of the mess
Nothing else to do

Do you really know?
Would you like to know?
What it feels like to be
Financially under attack
Can't afford the chicken
So have to buy the back

Now money run out
Can't even afford that
Have to contact the thugs on the block

Every day you sit and talk
About how we make guns bark
But have you tried to supply us with jobs?
Not even food to eat we have

A gunman in the scheme
Brilliant young man with 9 CXC's
But a job, he has none
So he takes up a gun
And go on a robbing spree

Do you really know how it feels?
To see him lying on the ground
Another life gone down
The norm in the ghetto.[5]

---

[5] Written when I was thirteen years old about the realities I saw going on around me.

UNFAIR YET?

Life is so unfair, some may say
But they have not heard half of the story
While some die of hunger and rot away
Others dance and prance in riches and glory
Some are homeless, battered and bruise
While you sit and complain about your third cruise

Life is so unfair
Do you even know what that means?
I have no right to say unfair
Because I've got clean air
Water, electricity, home, and food
And the clothes on my back
Are not worn and torn

Unfair is when you can't
Walk peacefully in the streets
Without getting harassed by cops
Or beat up by people's looks and thoughts

Unfair is when you can't get a job
Regardless of your qualifications
Because of your address
Being treated unfairly is to be
Ostracized, scorned, and teased
Because of financial instability

Unfair is how troops storm Africa
The richest continent on the earth
To steal their diamonds and mineral reserves
To leave them desolate and stained from bloodshed
To quiet and convince them that they are the poorest

Unfair is where refugees feel stuck
When war blazes up in their country
And they have to root up
Say goodbye to their home to find refuge
In a place they know not for safety's sake.[6]

---

[6] Written when I was fourteen years old about the inequality I saw: the poor versus the rich and powerful.

Pain

I can't take the pain
It's showering like the rain
It hurts just like heartache

It comes with such a force
That drives me to remorse
And holds me there

It sinks into my soul
And makes me feel so cold
Taking all my warmth away

If I dare to move
It comes with rejuvenated strength
It makes me feel so weak
And all the strength I seek
It has taken

My joy has been replaced
With sorrow upon my face
By its unpleasantness

Like a bee it stings
I try to sing
But singing is not enough

Because I can still feel
The pain like stainless steel
Penetrating through my flesh

No matter how hard I yelp
The pain still delves
Deeper and deeper

Praying on my knees
For the pain to cease
I ask for death to come quickly

As memories flash
And my life slowly passes
I cry with bitter tears

One special memory
It comes and stays
It does not fade
That of my beloved

Tears of joy spring to my eyes
As I realise
What is happening

For my pains ease
And my memories cease
At the moment

18 Years of Solitude

I begin to understand
What was said all along
My life's journey

Pain conquers anything
Almost everything
Except for love.[7]

---

[7] Written when I was fourteen years old. I started writing about menstrual cramps and it evolved into something different.

Trapped In Our Minds

Trapped in our minds
Knowing the truth
That it's wrong,
But still convincing ourselves
That it's right
Pleasing our flesh
Rather than unburdening
Our souls

We have all been
Trapped in our minds
Seeking pleasure
For ourselves
While the knowledge
Of truth
Fades away slowly

In the active mind
Where thoughts whirl
Around a central theme

Have we been trapped
Tryna figure out
The thoughts that erupt
Our conscience.[8]

---

[8] Written when I was fourteen years old about "forbidden sex," drawing from vicarious experiences.

Second Priority

"So, are you leaving?"
She asked casually
Searching for the answer she seeks
But a shrug of the shoulder was the response she gave
To the heart-breaking answer she received
She hid the pain all the while
Of how she felt like an abandoned child

For a heartless egocentric man was she abandoned
And put in the back of her mother's mind
For him her mother's world revolved
But for her own daughter she had no time
She always soaked it up
Then go to her favourite place to cry
Let out all her emotions
In a tree to the sky
The clouds knew her pain
The leaves her worries
But her mom never seemed to notice

Her mother's first priority
Was that distasteful man
Before him came not her daughter, not even God
She who called herself a Christian

She looked at it deeply
And cried some more
She cried and cried
Until her eyes were sore

This is it, she decided
She could not stay
She took one last look back
Packed her bags and ran away.[9]

---

[9] Written when I was fourteen years old. Feelings of abandonment when my mother's attention was turned to a man she was interested in, but who I did not like.

Limited

Word rush through my mind
In a supersonic way
Letters, sentences, and paragraphs
Stories and apologies
Flooded my head
But still nothing to say.[10]

---

[10] Written when I was fourteen years old about my inability to express when overwhelmed.

In His Mind

Cars, money, fame
That has always been the deal
The only things in life
For which he had zeal

Richness – his only goal
If even to sell his soul
Though he ever denies it
The half has never been told

How far will he go?
He doesn't eat what he grows
But seeks to reap
Of what he didn't sow

Soon he starts to lust
Collecting unjust
But God always prove to us
That man is just dust

And on he goes
Stepping on other's toes
To reach the top of the stairs
While instilling hatred and fears

He will stop at nothing
Until he gets what he wants
And so the devil's praise
He proclaims and chants

Almost there, just a month to go
He just knew he was gonna blow
His price was already paid
Now time to get gold
But the devil came early for his soul.[11]

---

[11] Written when I was fourteen years old. A poem about greed and materialism.

POVERTY

Hunger
Always whipping
Vicious slave master
Over poor unfortunate souls
Taking young girls solemn virginity
Leaving them scarred from
Selling their bodies
All because
Poverty.[12]

---

[12] Written when I was fourteen years old. A diamante done in literature class. Teacher said it was too "raw."

Broken Hearted

Scarred for life! That she was
When she saw the ungodly sight
Tears pierced her eyes,
And began to race down her grief-smitten face

Anger, disappointment, regret
Such understatements to what she felt
And heartbroken too weak a word.

The world around her disappeared
And she was all alone
Cold, shaken, terrified

The sky seems to spin endlessly above her
And the ground seems to shake fervently below her

And she was trying to hold on
To her integrity
To her heart
Before she broke apart
Anymore than the damage that was already done

Moon, stars, sky
They all could see
But would never understand
The pain she was feeling

More tears and even more
Kept bleeding down her face and scarred heart

Trying to emerge out of her sorrows
But could not
Seemed as if she was drowning

Fear took over her soul
She was afraid to face reality

The aching began and
The pains she was feeling
Had really just started
Why me?! Why me?!
She pleaded.

She lay on the ice-cold floor
Which evaporated all her warmth
And bathe herself in the freezing cold

Her heartbeat was so loud
She wanted it to stop
It was like a piercing scream to the ears
But she assured herself
That was not
And will never be the way

Trust disappeared and doubt came
Not a single soul would she trust again
Not only was her heart breaking
But fire consumed it
As her anger strengthened

Everything was senseless
Nothing mattered to her now
As she shuddered at the memory of
What broke her heart
Her sympathy went with the memory

Sorrow removed itself
And grief backed away
Self-pity stood afar off
And reality started to seep in

She made up her mind
Got up off the freezing floor
She wouldn't be helpless anymore

Tears still flowing
She took up a knife
Not her
But someone else
Had to die tonight.[13]

---

[13] Written when I was fourteen years old. Stemmed from feelings of anger and hurt from the actions of a family member.

SLEEP

World stands still
Watching you lay there
In your bed
Just resting your head
God only knows
Who you're dreaming of
And what's on your mind
So you
Sleep on

Time comes and goes
But you don't know a thing
That's going on around you
You're deep in sleep and missing
Everything that comes your way
But you
Sleep on
Hypnotized by dreams
Enticed by sleep
You'd stay there

The whole day and night
If you could
Cuz you want to
Sleep on

But if you sleep on
How do you expect
The world to rise and come to its best
You make me upset
You are a sleeping drunk head
You need to hear the trumpet
Blowing, calling to you
It's so loud, answer!
Some people say you need
To wake up and smell the coffee
But it's too late
It's evening already
So no coffee is here
Only a glass of sour lemonade.[14]

---

[14] Written when I was fourteen years old. A poem started as an ode to sleep, which at the time I was addicted to. I was oversleeping a lot.

My Story

Been through a lot
Probably not where you've been
Down a different path
I trod

Poverty & low self-esteem
Probably not where you've been,
So let me tell you
It's a lot.

We have never ever been on the same path
So how dare you try to put blame on me
For being what you're not?
"Rock stone at river bottom
Doesn't feel sun hot at river top"
We might meet at the same crossroads
But don't you dare think
You know me or what I've been through

I may seem too quiet
But silent river runs deep
And don't bother to judge
Cause you see me everyday
But you still don't know my story

I'm not an open book, so you won't see
What I'm about by just looking at me
I may not share your views
I even might, but you won't know
Cause you can't read my mind

Just like how
You'll never know my views
Or what I think
You'll never know who I am
Until I let you into my world,
My web of thoughts
My secret imaginations, my pillow
My stance, my reason for dance
My problems, my life, my mind, my actions
Mine! My story, not yours![15]

---

[15] Written when I was fourteen years old.

Unbreakable Bond

Deep breath
Deep breath
That's all they said
But I was busy
Listening to the
Pounding in my head

Speechless
Speechless
That's how I remained
When my pulse
Kept getting faster
With the pounding still untamed

Then you came into this world
Such a beautiful girl
Tears came to my eyes
When I first heard you cry
As they wiped you clean
Nothing could stand between our hearts
The bond is still unbreakable.[16]

---

[16] Written when I was fourteen years old about the bond between mother and child.

THE CRUSH

Gotta get him off my mind
Cause it's not worth the try
Not this time!
He can't even see that I'm falling for him
Or probably that's what I think.
What if he understands?
Or what if he doesn't know I exist?
I never thought about it.
What if he knows me
But just doesn't like me like I want him to?
Or what if he hates my guts
And I upset his stomach?

I just realized
I'm saying too much "what-ifs"
What if I die
And it's all because of madness?
Because I'm sitting here
Tryna figure out his feelings for me

Instead of finding my own identity.
What if he loves me
More than I can tell?
Oh, I'd love that very well
Right now I don't know where I stand
I don't think I stand a chance
But how will I ever know
Unless
I give it my best shot.[17]

---

[17] Written when I was fourteen years old. A poem about teenage crush.

INSECURITY

Beautiful, beautiful girl
Sitting there
Staring in the mirror
Wanting to change the way you look
Can't you see?
You're perfect!

Young girl
You got your life ahead of you
No time for regrets
Or putting self down
You destroy yourself
Seeing what other people "see"
They must be blind
Cause you're beautiful
A masterpiece
God's workmanship

No need to feel embarrassed
Hold your head up
Stick your chin out

18 Years of Solitude

Why do you think they talk?
They're jealous
Jealous of your beauty
So why the insecurity?
Insecurity?!
That should never be in your vocabulary
Lowering your self-esteem
Doesn't work either
Just look in the same mirror
This time
Don't focus on your 'flaws'
This time, explore your beauty
Throw away your insecurity.[18]

---

[18] Written when I was fourteen years old. A poem written after realizing I was insecure about my appearance.

Sky Of Battle

The dark clouds of grey
Swiftly drift away
Underlay the clouds of white
Covering the light blue sky
A perfect scenery
Then these drops of rain out of nowhere
Settling on my windowpane
My heart's desire is to make tears resurface
But I can't
My heart is a frozen stone
Hard and cold
Ever since…

Sympathy hates me
Compassion and I are sworn enemies
Conscience has been burnt
Now I am ready
To face my rival,
Love.[19]

---

[19] Written when I was fourteen years old, trying to explain my feelings based off the weather.

LISTENING TO MUSIC?

As I lie on my bed, I think about you
Are the words you're telling me true?
Do you really mean what you say?
You told me that day,
You love me
I can't help but wonder
The last day of school in December
Was it fate for us to socialize
For the very first time?
When I saw the longing in your eyes
To claim me as your prize
When I felt my lips droop from
Smiling at you and everything you said

I don't know how
But when I'm with you
I feel inadequate, yet confident
I feel so alive
Like before you I wasn't living life
The cries of my heart keep deafening me

Pounding in my heart, loud in my ears
Take the chance, even if you fall
Once you give him your all
Show him the music in you

But now I'm thinking, what should I do?
Are the words you're telling me true?
About how you love and how you care?
Should I really hear you out?
You said you'll never hurt me. Ever!
You said you'll be true to me
You said, you said
You said....
So many things you said
Are you just filling up my head?
Or do you mean it?
Should I believe you?
My instincts are telling me to
But then, they could be wrong
The only advice I can follow
Is that of my heart
Which told me from the start
Take the chance, even if you fall
After giving him your all
And showing him the music in you

I don't know what to do
Are the words you're telling me true?
It could all be a lie

18 Years of Solitude

A convenient scheme
To get me in your web
And rather than doing what you said
You break my heart instead

I know I want you
Of that I'm sure
But I don't know if I can trust you more
It's not an issue of you being the problem
It's me and you might even be the solution
I'm falling for you
I have fallen for you
So, I'm bombarded with illusions and delusions
And I don't know how to sort em
What is real, what is true
From what is not
This knot on my string of sanity
Is roping for me to
Lose my mind over you

Are the words you're telling me true?
Of course I'm sure I want you
To be the one I trust
To be mine
But I'm not sure you hear the music in me
Or understand my irrelevant rhyme.[20]

---

[20] Written when I was fourteen years old. A poem stemming from an actual crush.

Happiness Is For Humans

This was the day the devil almost won
He didn't get my distasteful life
But he shook my soul
I'd rather if he took my life
What purpose do I serve in this
Cold, corrupt, complicated world
If my soul cannot stand on its own
My temple of white has transformed
Into the colour of death
Maimed by a loss, by THE LOSS
The loss of the last cause to live
The cost?
Love, friendship, connection
Now all I'm left with is music

Dark, heart-wrenching, soul-touching music
It probably would be darker
If it was able to touch my soul
But it can't, for I am darker
I have no soul

18 Years of Solitude

I have nothing to lose
No more can be lost
For all is already lost for me
Then why do I live?
I live to remember until I die
Until I am lost
Lost in the swirling ashes of death
And the dust of forgetting
If it were possible
For now, I cannot forget
I always remember, especially this day
Filled with memories of things I die to forget
For remembering them is a depressant
Sinking me deeper and deeper
Until I am fully immersed
In a world of blackness

Unheard voices, unanswered calls
Unfelt presences, unseen visitors
A parody of reality
Insensitive senses
Unfound heartbeat
Deafening silence
But for now, I am just dark
I am not yet prepared for the blackness

The devil almost won
He didn't get my life
But he shook my soul

At least if he did it,
I wouldn't be the living dead
This was the day
I sold my soul
For a memory
Keeping me alive
But killing me slowly.[21]

---

[21] Written when I was fifteen years old. A poem about sad dates and memories.

Night's Rest

As I curl in the middle of this bed crying
I'd like to think that everything will be okay
But this swirl of thoughts
Have carried my problems to stay

Out of a dungeon so deep
My problems come awake
They rise until
I'm conscious of the heartache

This bed is too big, much too big for me
For colours and patterns of loneliness is all I see

Past, present, and what-if's mix
To make a most bitter combination of dark thoughts
Filled with worrying and frustration

Another sleepless night, another fallen tear
Knowing I'll spend the time wishing I didn't care
Mortal mind wondering where immortal thoughts are
Trespassing in another state of mind
Somewhere far

Far from reality and the ironies of life
Ignoring the call back to the present
Where life is just a thing
Never for me meant

Coldness surrounds the heart
Of the body that shivers
Laying in the heart of the dark
While tears become salt rivers

An endless prayer prayed in silence
Of the long night to be saved from the pestilence

Swollen red eyes stare at the dim moon
Hoping day will come soon
Why is it done ever so often?

So many sleepless nights
So many tears cried
Where bitterness bred
And deception came alive

Where the darkness envelopes
The faintest of forms
In this long lonely
All night storm

Not a storm of rain and thunder
But of sorrow and
Happiness drifting asunder

The storm rages through the night
Until dawn, the first peep of light
When my wind of emotions will cease
If by then I haven't cried myself to sleep
Again.[22]

---

[22] Written when I was fifteen years old. A poem about sleepless nights.

Cold

When everyone around you
Is humid or warm
And you are shivering from the cold
The endless torturing cold that nobody feels
But you

You try to explain but they,
They just don't understand
And you wish you'd have someone
To hold your hand
To let you know you are not alone
To tell you they know what you're feeling
And you can go through it together

Even my worst enemy I'd settle for
To know it's not only my heart
Being slowly frozen by the frost and cold
That haunts my every waking moment
And drags me out of sleep
But I'd rather face it alone

Although I cry for a companion
I'd wish this fate on no man

Immune to warmth
Trembling, shaking cold.[23]

---

[23] Written when I was fifteen years old. A poem about how I feel.

Compliment

Someone gave me a compliment
And I tried to smile
But the smile wasn't forming
Two seconds later
A tear is rolling down my cheek

Why does my heart do this to me?
I've never had mood swings nor PMS
And I don't think I am stressed
But what could it be
That makes me cry
When I should smile
What matter is my heart
Bringing to the forefront of my mind
Out of where darkness
And the subconscious lies

I can't say I'm overwhelmed
I have no reason to be
All along I was "happy"
Having fun, so carefree

Then all of a sudden
This teardrop appears
Causing all my problems
To bang down my heart's door.

But I won't let them in
No, not at all
Unless I'm prepared to lose it all
My sanity, reason to smile
My ability to look someone straight in the eye
And tell them I'm alright.[24]

---

[24] Written when I was fifteen years old.

Struggling On

Cracking at every high point in her life
She struggles on
Beaten, depressed, alone
Life may have its way
But in the end
Nothing compares to the experience she has
The deaths, the sicknesses, the family feuds, the stress
But indeed, she is blessed
For she still stands on her own two feet
Although struggling

Never has she once thought about giving up
And look at her now
So graceful, yet so strong
Unexplainable is the fire that keeps her going
Where is it from?
Her life is a barrage of inequality
Friends are treated no better
Under one umbrella they fall

Her anger is incomprehensible
How does she do it?
Keep calm when discrimination
And insults are thrown from all sides
No one has ever been lulled
Into her innermost thoughts and emotions
Her heart won't let it be
For it is guarded by the perception
That no-one is trustworthy
No one knows
No one cares
No one ever will.[25]

---

[25] Written when I was fifteen years old. A poem about the strength of a woman. Inspired by my mother.

From My Distance

My love, I wept for you today
I cried when everyone else went to play
My body was there, but not my mind
For it lingered on you the whole time

I can't believe you did this to me
Oh, if you could see
See that I'm the right one for you
I have loved you, been faithful and true
And this is what it has come to?

Another girl's tongue down your throat
Another of your girlfriends I will loathe
But if you just open up your eyes
You will see my love in disguise

When all is said and done
I will still be the one
The one who cherishes your every smile
The way you laugh, and your captivating eyes

The one who knows everything about you
Yet the one whom you refuse
Soon, my love, you will realise
And by that time
I'll have no more tears left to cry

But I'll still be waiting
Waiting for you, my love.[26]

---

[26] Written when I was fifteen years old. An on-the-spot poem request.

The Album

Sweet melodies fill my ear
A particular song comes to mind
Just by thinking of you
And all you left behind

The sweetest of melodies
But the worst song ever
For how it reminds me of when we severed

The distasteful words that left your mouth
Were nothing to be pleased with
Your attitude was worse
Treating me like I ain't worth it

How it pained my heart to see
The one who told me he'd never leave
Was packing his bags while ignoring me

I'd like to think he cared
If even a little
But that's just wishful thinking
Because he never cared from the beginning

18 Years of Solitude

I should've known
All that glitters isn't gold
But that didn't cross my mind
When admiring how he was bold
Fun-loving, carefree
I should've realised he wouldn't care for me

But what's done is done,
It's all dead and gone.
I just wish these memories
Wouldn't keep on

When a heart breaks, it don't break even
That's what they say
So, while I'm here in misery
You're probably partying like it's yo birthday

I can only imagine now
What you think of me
The girl you thought was classy
Is now under your feet
You got what you wanted, so you left
Whose heart are you going to steal next?[27]

---

[27] Written when I was fifteen years old. An on-the-spot poem request.

Hopeless

With feeble hearts and crippled minds
Conjuncture of hopes that cannot be defined
An ignorance of the thickening line
Between lost and gone

Red lights flash and sirens wail,
But still to no avail
Our spirits are not set free
From the effects of poverty

Times and seasons come and go
Yet still we will always know
The sun doesn't shine for us to make hay,
Only to survive another day

Nothing tried, nothing done
Those times are already gone
Goals have evaporated, scorched by the sun
Dreams have faded before they've began
But still we do this thing
Surviving, but not at all living

Half-beating hearts sound our arrival
Souls weakened by despair
Faintly lit eyes that search and search
For a hope that was never there
Optimism comfort only fools
But fools we are not
Only deprived of all the benefits
The rich and educated got.[28]

---

[28] Written when I was fifteen years old. A poem about the hopelessness of my people due to poverty and other destructive cycles.

Mental Slavery

Mental slavery is a helluva ting
Kept in bondage by your own self
Platting every chain link
With every negative thought you think
For the oppression of your soul
Drinking yourself to misery
Saying that you can't
When you know from your heart
Every obstacle from start to end
You can overcome
But because you don't believe
That's where the slaver is conceived.[29]

---

[29] Written when I was sixteen years old.

DECLARING THE PROMISE

Shouting it
There's nothing funny about it
So why you laughing
Like I'm performing
Not a stand-up comedian
No jokes coming out of my mouth
So, won't you stop laughing
And just hear me out

The earth is the Lord's
And the fullness thereof
You are not your own
So, you can't just go about your business
Like you don't know
Cuz now you know
You belong to the Lord
Delight in prayers and trust in His Word
He is waiting for you to stop by
Even just to kneel and say hi
Amen

That's a start
Then you have to repent in your heart
You know the things you are doing wrong
The sins you've committed,
The races you've won unfairly
The thoughts you thought
And the times you laughed
When you should have helped instead
Yes, you know them
Sometimes you look back and frown
Now's the time to turn your life around

You know who created you
So why do you fail to praise him?
It's not enough to just believe He is God
That can't take away your sins
It's not your clothes that matter
So just come as you are
It's your heart and thoughts He wants
But children of the King

Dresses as royalty, princesses, and princes
You know your conscience trouble you sometimes
When you plan to do something
Considered evil in God's sight
So why not listen to that voice
The one from deep within
It's the voice of the Holy Spirit
Warning us against sin

Don't you know we were made for one reason?
No matter what time, day or season
It is our duty to worship the Most High
After all, for us Jesus came and died

I know you want to party and have "fun"
After all, you are not old
But what does it profit a man
To gain this whole world and lose his soul?

Nothing, my people
It profits nothing
So, are you willing to give it up for Jesus?
The partying, the cursing, the skimpy clothes?
Or do you prefer those?
I'm not the writer, only the messenger
And it's not my decision, it's yours
Just to let you know
Jesus loves you
Even if you say no to His will
He will be waiting still.[30]

---

[30] Written when I was sixteen years old. A poem written to spread the gospel of Christ.

Self-Righteous

Show me mercy and I'll show you pain
Give me grace; I'll make you do it again

Oh, I know you can do no wrong
And I know how you are
Still I see the good in you
And I hope you can see good in me too
After all I've been through
After all I said
After I kicked you to the curb
When you wanted to be in my bed

You see, I should've known you would've gone around
Turning trouble upside down with your big mouth
Acting like a clown
Hyping up like the clerk of the town
But No!
Noooooooo!
Don't you see how petty you seem?
When you make up stuff only possible in your dreams?

But then again it could've been
Only if you could've seen the way it was supposed to be
You were supposed to be gentle to me

I could've loved you like you wanted me to
But I couldn't play by your rules
If things were different you would see then
What I meant when I say: You weren't mine anyway

Because one street is closed
And the other is one way
So, what we had, had to be left at bay
To stray
And what I saw is not there now
Did it all vanish somehow?
Or maybe I'm delusional
A patient of hallucination

It ain't possible for you to change that quick
So, either I was blind or you were always like this
Arrogant and untruthful
Spreading rumours all about
But one day you'll see when I'm out, I'm out

And I'm out
I'm not in
Not in your life again
So, say goodbye to what could've been
And stop spreading lies, it ain't happening

Unless in your dreams
Cuz you're hallucinating
Either high or you drinking
Cuz I'm not the one to be your bride
You see, I'm different from what you need
And what you want
I can't give
No
I can't give
Maybe you're not listening
I can't give you what you want!

It ain't in my power
Not this minute or hour
Or any other time you want me to sublime
From ice to gas in a few minutes
I'm not like that.
If I'm ice, I'm ice
And I'll have to turn to liquid
Before I vaporize
I ain't flash
I can't do it in a sec
But I'm gas and I ain't turning to nothing else

I'm invisible but always there
I'm in your every breath of air
I surround you everywhere
I'll only go if you say so
But it was obvious you wanted me to go

18 Years of Solitude

From the words you said and the actions you showed
I felt so disrespected, you know

And every time my mind flashes back
I keep thinking, why would he do that?!
And I say it's obvious, he just wants what he wants
To have fun, get wild and gallivant
Ain't nothing about how I would feel
When your true self revealed
Like a mouse in a spinning wheel

Turning and spinning, low and high
No real direction, just a ride
And oh, how it would've ended
With wheel flat on its side and the mouse shaken
For how tedious it was to stop
Opposed to how the ride started
And, my dear, that was why we parted

So alas now
Make no more stories of me
Cuz it gives me something bad to think of you
When the good is all I see.[31]

---

[31] Written when I was seventeen years old. A poem written about someone I had high regards for, who distorted the truth, after I closed off communication for my wellbeing.

Joyful Noise

I'm gonna fly away
On the wings of the morning
Searching for a brighter day

I'm gonna reach the stars
And capture them in conquest
To bring them down for you
And win your heart
I'm gonna search the world
High and low and all around
Until I find the one that is mine

Then I'm gonna set my heart in peace
To live and love and laugh
The way it is supposed to be
Happy at last

Make you believe what I believe
And you'll see what I can see
And we'll be bonded equally

And our hearts will be set free
By the love that rides the wind
And flows from deep within
And cast out all our fears
And only bring joyful tears

I want that love
I want it now
But you know I ain't ready for it
I want the peace that comes with knowing
You are the only one for me

And I will sing
And I will shout
And I will clap
And I will dance
For I have found the one for me
And this love will set us free
Through all eternity.[32]

---

[32] Written when I was seventeen years old. A poem about anticipating the "love" that everyone speaks of.

Refuse

What did I do to deserve
All the neglect and curse?
What did I ever say
To make you treat me this way?
Is that how I'm perceived in your eyes?
One worthy of abuse and despise?
Am I to you such a reproach
That for my demise you wait and encroach?

I always thought I was a humble one
Downplayed the victories I've won
Never exalted myself at all
Ran to you each time you called

Been there for you through thick and thin
Dragged you out of the different situations you fell in
Mothering your "one and only" child
Cleared your name of all wrongs and guile
And for a while
Just a little time

18 Years of Solitude

You got me thinking
You would do the same for me

Either you've changed
Or I was blind
My eyes being clouded by the love I had inside
That I still have for you
Even though you've treated me so
Harsh, cruel, like an old dirty rag
Love in my heart for you is all I have

Some would say I'm foolish, others bland
But they just wouldn't understand
My heart fails me when I try to hate you
Is it because I overrate you?
My tongue ties when I try to curse you
Because I know I really don't want to
And when I'm considering going away
Every single cell in my body convinces me to stay
Even though I'm hurting by the things you say
The games you play, the way you treat me

I remember every single time
My eyes were black and blue
Or red and swollen because of you
The days when my blood painted the tiles
And my bruises craved for balming oil
I remember all the nights you never came home

But staggered in at dawn
After waiting up for you all night
No strength to argue, just to yawn

The cry of an oppressed soul
Inhabiting a battered broken body.[33]

---

[33] Written when I was seventeen years old. A poem about women holding on to toxic relationships in spite of domestic abuse.

CRY

Crystal drops meet the sheet
In dozens, one behind the other
A river path made on my cheeks
With clouded thoughts that make me shiver

The dark room invaded by my needless emotions
Lingering in the air above
My sobs and whispers and confessions
Spoken softer than the flap of wings of a dove

A steady beat playing on the drums in my chest
Loud and on-point, and never seeming to rest
A soft tremble on my lips
And they do lie, unlike my hips

I've been a strong girl
A bold statue for all to see
Now I don't know if I can take it anymore

A little weakness every once in a while
Doesn't mean I'm not strong
Only means I've been pretending all along

Feelings and emotions are supposed to be felt
That's why we are made with a heart and skin
But how can you feel the rhythm
If you refuse to let the music in

Eternities pass between each breath
What a fool I've been
My pride blocking the way
I should've been there

But all that's left to do is being done
For I am crying
Next task: moving on

I must take the next big chance
I will be happy
I will make them happy
I will not cry
But I may shed some tears of joy.[34]

---

[34] Written when I was seventeen years old. A poem written during one of my meltdowns.

THE BRICK WALL

A young black woman
Scarred by her past
Living in a vacuum
No air to breath, no company to last
All hope forgotten
Protected by the great wall
She builds around herself
Warding off emotions, hurt and pain
Admirers strain to gain her trust
So, they lust after her heart
Beyond the bricks standing tall
Protected by the wall
She exists in the vacuum
Comforted in her safety
Knowing no one could break through
Yet she was dying inside.[35]

---

[35] Written when I was seventeen years old. A poem written about my defence mechanism in not letting anyone close to me and being heavily guarded.

IDK

From your wavy black hair
To your long feet
There is nothing I would change

You smile and my whole world lights up
A wonder wrought by those thin pink lips of yours
Showing your large, cloud-white, perfect set of teeth

He doesn't really love me, I tell myself
But every time you turn those
Large, innocent, winkling eyes on me
I think differently
The adoration in your eyes is no mistake
As you try to utter it with the words you say
At other times, the longing they show
Pierce me to my soul
When you stare intensely at me and
I read every thought through your blinks

I remember you sitting on the desktop
Facing me with your back arched and
Your long legs dangling close to the ground

The frustration in your face arguing with me
And how it changed to puzzlement and then
To bewilderment and back to frustration
Trying to get me to be yours

Every emotion painstakingly written
On your dark, handsome face
The intensity of your cologne enveloping the air
Inching me closer to you
Smelling like seduction

Do you remember? The song you used to sing
Jigging next to me at the back of the class

The gentleness of your hand caressing mine
Haunts me at nights
How it erased all my fears and worries
And made me think just about us against the world

Melodies would swarm my mind
Every time you appeared in my field of vision
I don't even know if I know why I love you
But I'd be a fool not to

A sea of emotions engulfs me
Every time I think of you

A tall dark handsome guy you are,
But that's not all
Your personality is what made you my star,
No doubt about it

So protective of me
You were my soldier
Fighting for my affection and attention
Keeping me out of harm's way
A strong soldier

But you were weak for me
Weak to my touch
Weak to my kiss
Weak to me

Everything I asked for
You gave to me
Some in full and some in part
Like, honestly,
I didn't ask for much
Cuz I had all I needed
When you were sitting next to me

Amusement covered your face
When you played with my hair
And when I was far away
I felt your heart of despair

I never meant to hurt you
By not giving you enough of
My love, thoughts, feelings
Yours were overflowing
An ocean I kept drowning in

Green with jealousy
You were not yet my ogre
But you showed your displeasure
When other males I gushed over
Or even talked to
Or just to simply touch
I guess seeing another male beside me
Was for you just too much

You strived to be a rare flower
The only one I admired
Of course you were not
But were the only one I desired

And I wanted to tell you
And show you so bad
You understood all my thoughts
Every single technicality
And saw beyond the
Voluptuous body a heart
Of genuinity
And I saw yours
The way you were passionate about me
Gave me every reason to be about you
And I was

Why couldn't I just show it
For all the world to see?
Like you did

I remember you putting
Your head on my shoulder
And all the world seemed to be at peace
I remember how I got you excited
When we kissed in that booth
It was funny to me

You used to drive me crazy
Trying to focus on my academics
With my mind always wandering
Back to you

We would talk on the phone for hours
And it scared me
Before you came along
Nothing lessened my sleep

You would act goofy
And I'm always the shy girl
But it always seemed to be a different world
Where I was happy
I was yours and you were mine
Our desires intertwined
And I know
I knew from the day
That you would change my life

And I hate the way I feel
When I realized what I lost
And I can't stand how often

I think of you, but I like to
I like you
I loved you
I love you
And I don't know why.[36]

---

[36] Written when I was seventeen years old. A poem reminiscing on my somewhat first experience of romance in High School.

Limbo

I know nothing!
That much I know
I'm just an inadequate girl
Living in a fantasy world
One full of dreams and castles and happiness
Illuminated by the light of mystery
Wishing for a companion to join the tale
To come sing along to the
Half broken melody I croak
Through cracked dry lips and a sore throat
Thirsting for love
Scorched from loneliness
A harmony to be completed
But no one to croak with me
To dance to the off-beat rhythm
Of this severed heart
Sorrowing through the darkest hours of the night
And the brightest minutes of the day

18 Years of Solitude

My mind is rotting
From the sweet thoughts of companionship
And carnage of the hope which was once mine
Soon my heart will rot too
From inactivity, no inhibitors, no visitors
No trespassers, no one, nothing
The seas roar my anger
And the winds howl for my lost cause
A heart borne in vain
To breathe contempt on faith
And pour scorn on hope
Nothing is ever free
A price has to be paid
For laughter and joy are not merit goods
Preserved by a deep reserve of gloom
Frozen by indifference
Deep down in my soul.[37]

---

[37] Written when I was seventeen years old. A poem about loneliness.

THE LAST PRAYER

Why?
What did he do so bad?
Oh, mighty God,
To deserve a death like this?
Cold and bloody, leaving dirt
And strands of dried grass on his lips
His deathbed made on the tough ground
Eyes open wide with shock and disbelief
As the pounding of heart gushes all the blood
From the slowing heart of gold
Through thirsty veins to the ground
Via the hole in the back of his head
Pierced through by a bullet of steel.

He comes to the realization,
Realization is his eyes, the way he stares
Up into the cold night
Like he finally understands
Figured out an unfathomable mystery
And it hit him right in time to say his last prayers

And with a new understanding
He turns his head up to the heavens
A night full of stars covered by gloom
And he searches for the moon
And in the moment of time
He says the words in his heart
And with a jolt his prayer stops
The pounding stops
The fear stops
The fluttering stops
The blinking stops
The noise of crickets stops
The seeing stops
The sky ends
The moon stops
The star stops
The dogs shut up
The cold stops
The air stops
The breath stops
The lungs stop
The brain stops
The night stops
The light bend
And another life ends
With eyes still open
Iris clear as an ocean
With a light brown sheen

Still staring sincerely into the unseen
Mouth half open
Stopped in mid whisper
And the dogs howl
To bring to the site people from all around
To bear witness of the
Death of the wandering prayer whisperer

At least, that's how I think it goes
But would it be a shame
If he never even got the chance
To call the LORD'S NAME

To lay his final request
At the feet of his heavenly Father
And make confessions he should have done ages before
What if not even a sound left his mouth?
And like that he went down
His light flickered out with a fatal blow
And he didn't even know.[38]

---

[38] Written when I was seventeen years old. A poem prompted by the murder of a community member.

Reflection

I thought I could forget
Shame on me
For my happiness is imprisoned in the memory

Sometimes I wish I had died that night
Than to live in this light
Scrutinized and criticized, and eventually ostracized

But it is not that, that bothers me
It is not the criticisms and scrutiny
It is not the rejection
It is what I see when I look at my reflection
Every time I look, I see you.[39]

---

[39] Written when I was seventeen years old. A poem written after staring in the mirror for a long time.

Unforeseen

I'll write the histories of the lives I never knew
And take them to be mine
The thoughts of lost souls I'll reveal
I will be the voice of the hopeless and the weak
Those whose light reclined
I not I
They will live through me
And all the voices in my head you will come to know
But then your life I will unravel too
For I need not know what is happening now
Just that it does
Another chronicle written
About a boy I've never seen,
A girl I've never known,
A world I've never been to
But I know it exists.

The turmoil of the strong
And the struggles of the rich
The weaknesses of the powerful

18 Years of Solitude

I have heard them all in the song of the wind
And the chirp of birds
I have seen their lives in the dreams of the night
And slid in the clouds
I know them not.
But I know
I might not know you.
But I know
Just know
Whatever you are going through, someone knows.[40]

---

[40] Written when I was seventeen years old. This is how I feel when I write poetry from my imagination, almost as if I am seeing beyond the natural and somewhat prophesying through poetry.

Dreams

I lay at night in that state
Not knowing where I want to be
And off my mind floats to a place of serenity
I don't know who decides
Far too many times
I've found myself running,
Running from murderers and monsters
Running towards home
Running into people
I have never met or known

Sometimes it feels like multiples of eternity
At other times milliseconds
But I've come to notice when I'm there
I never have a weapon in my possession
At times so real
Unlike times when I'm swimming in the air

I know mine is strange
So many receipts of glares

18 Years of Solitude

When I try to explain
My refuge they may be
But never my sanctuary

The unknown brought to knowledge
The known brought to remembrance
In my dreams.[41]

---

[41] Written when I was seventeen years old. I experienced a lot of real, weird, frightening, and prophetic dreams that were weighing on my mind.

Black Rain

Mist surrounds the earth
And with each passing second
Disperses into the dark
Each pure crystalline droplet
Announce its arrival with a spat!

As ripples form across
The surface of the weeping sea
One after the other
They fall from the heavens
Creating a song of wet melodies
And falling beats
In the black night
Lulling them to sleep
All except she
She feels the pull of her heart
Hears the song and glorifies it
The distant rumbling of the cloud pacifies
Tip

18 Years of Solitude

Tip

Tip

Tip

Tip

A mêlée of thoughts in between

Like arrows falling from the sky

They pierce the earth and seep through

Like dark messengers carrying words of sorrow

Yet, there is joy

Each drop brings despair

Yet hope is brought

Specks of white wrestle against a constant black

Never-ending backdrop

But bleed as they become

Lost in the blackness.[42]

---

[42] Written when I was seventeen years old. A poem about how I feel when rain falls at night.

Her Mind

A maze of precautions and assumptions
One she doesn't try to solve or exit
For there is so much consideration given
To how to walk and where to sit

So much precision and decisions
Ripple through her thoughts
But is flooded by insecurity and jealousy

Swirling like snow in the wind
Are the indifference and arguments she holds
Cold as ice to the bone
And stone hard it makes the veins

But through the intricacies
And around the bends
Over stumbling blocks of information
One will find that her mind
Is pretty much like a shadow

18 Years of Solitude

You cannot see it clearly
And you cannot sway it
She is stubborn in her arguments

Such strong reasoning she possesses
And indomitable thoughts
But just the wooing of a lover
And the strong wall crumbles and falls

Like a puzzle, many seek to figure out
Her thought processes
But that is revealed not even to
The ones she relates the best.[43]

---

[43] Written when I was seventeen years old. A poem about a woman's mind.

Flirt

I should've kissed you
I really wanted to
I'm sure you could see it on my face

No doubt you were dying to
I could see it in your eyes
Like a fire kindled
Burning calm and sweet
Then blazes up
To the sound of your heartbeat
And you stare at me
And make my eyelids flutter
And my modesty goes numb.[44]

---

[44] Written when I was seventeen years old.

The Black Woman's Heart

Leave no stone unturned
Everything in the path must be burned
Burnt! Not like the orange of autumn leaves
Or the colour of our skin
But like ashes pressed deep within the earth,
Stomped under our feet

No, we will not accept defeat
To neither gravity nor our foes
We will rise after crushing
Every single one who oppose

And not by fear we say these words
But through tears, blood, sweat, and lessons learned
Trust no one! Not even yourself
And so, without hope we start this journey
Not expecting to find an ally
And if we do, we shrug them off
As one who schemes and is quick to lie

We trod alone with disdain
To those who say
We will die as lone wolves

We aren't prepared to die
But we are prepared to face death
With blows of our axes, we will dismantle
Its head from its neck
And if it chooses to return the favour
We will go down bold as ever
Alone
A sole warrior
Never envious of those with company
For we had ours present in our minds
Visible to no man, never falling behind
But leading us through our conquest
Head strong

The only companion we ever know
The only faithful one
To me, myself, and I
Miss Trust was never wrong
She told us
Leave no stones unturned
Everything must burn
Never fall prey to the charmer

A black woman's heart is a lone warrior.[45]

---

[45] Written when I was seventeen years old. A poem about women who are not easily wooed and have trust issues.

Ridden

Oh, what a fool I would've been
If I didn't give him a chance
If I didn't let him in
For now, I think he is the fuel to my beating heart

Oh, how wonderful love is
And he is the recipient of all of mine
There is no other such mortal that lives on my mind

Unlike all the other times before
This time it's genuine
It is definitely not infatuation
Or obsession to begin with
I feel so happy he has my heart
I know he won't break it
Maybe I've been ridden by devils from hell
Well, I guess that makes it easier to identify an angel
Certainly, he is the one

My angel.[46]

---

[46] Written when I was seventeen years old. A poem about young love.

LET ME BE

You don't have to rally around me
Or congratulate my victory
I'm not asking you to bow down
After all, for you I have no crown

It is needless to give me praise
With your heart twisted like a maze
Don't want you to be a hypocrite
To lie and say what you don't mean
Just give me space
I'm begging for it
To company with hearts and minds that are clean
Oh, for God's sake
Won't you just let me be![47]

---

[47] Written when I was seventeen years old. A poem expressing my annoyance at pretenders around me.

This Melody

This melody flows on the wind
Needless of a harmony
Like the drops of rain descending in a formed puddle
So beautiful, so simple
On scales so high
It touches the sky
And set back down to trace our hearts

This melody glides on the oceans
Never missing a wave
Like the perfect timing of a surfer
Dodging and landing
Skilfully set
Smoothly over our emotions it sails
And claims that of its own
Oh, I would have never known that sound

Now I'm left singing this melody
My heart has joined in
I can't refrain

This melody has broken the walls
Has shattered the glass case that held me captive
This melody has freed me
This melody
Love.[48]

---

[48] Written when I was seventeen years old. A poem about my expression of love.

ANGER

Each beat brings me closer
To my breaking point
Hurried and strong
It pounds against my chest
Mingled in my blood
Dispersed through my veins
Yet strongly characterised in my eyes
And rushes to my brain
This shall be the death of me
A red hot fire kindles in the pit of my stomach
And the flames quickly rise with each breath I take
My grip tightens and my body shakes
Steam push from my nostril and ears
My fury ends with drops of tears.[49]

---

[49] Written when I was seventeen years old.

About the Author

Moné is a free thinker and soulful writer, who serves God passionately in diverse ways. She was born and raised in St. Catherine, Jamaica where she currently resides and is an accountant by profession. When not writing poetry, she enjoys reading, dancing, and climbing trees.

www.ingramcontent.com/pod-product-compliance
Lightning Source LLC
Chambersburg PA
CBHW071715040426
42446CB00011B/2072